All the
Company
of
Heaven

All the Company of Heaven

*Compiled by
Meryl Doney*

**Regina Press
New York**

This edition published 2000 by Regina Press,
10 Hub Drive, Melville, NY 11747, USA
ISBN 0-88271-728-6

Published in association with
National Gallery Publications,
5/6 Pall Mall East, London SW1Y 5BA

All illustrations reproduced courtesy of the
Trustees of the National Gallery, London

10 9 8 7 6 5 4 3 2 1 0

Originally published and copyright © 1999
by Lion Publishing plc, Sandy Lane West,
Oxford, England

A catalogue record for this book is available
from the British Library

Typeset in 11/14 Caslon OldFace
Printed and bound in Singapore

If I give away all my possessions,
and if I hand over my body to be burned,
but do not have love, I gain nothing.

Saint Paul

Introduction

Therefore with Angels and Archangels,
and with all the company of heaven,
we laud and magnify thy glorious Name;
evermore praising thee, and saying:
Holy, holy, holy, Lord God of hosts,
heaven and earth are full of thy glory.
The Book of Common Prayer

Taken from the prayer at the heart of the
Holy Communion Service, the phrase 'all
the company of heaven' describes the joyful
saints in heaven, who join with all believers
to offer their worship to God.

This book is a celebration of the dedicated
and sometimes astonishing lives of men and
women of God, beautifully illustrated with
details from paintings in the National Gallery
collection in London.

Andrew

Feast day: November 30th

Fisherman, brother of Simon Peter and follower of John the Baptist, Andrew was one of the first of the twelve disciples to encounter Jesus. He is known for his practical faith and has often been depicted bringing people to Jesus. It is said that he preached the gospel as far as Byzantium before being crucified at Patras in Achaia in AD 60. As a result of the legend that his bones were taken to Scotland in the eighth century, Andrew became the patron saint of Scotland.

He found his brother Simon and said to him, 'We have found the Messiah.' He brought Simon to Jesus.
The Gospel of John

Gaudenzio Ferrari,
Saint Andrew (?)

Benedict

Feast day: July 11th

Born in Italy around AD 480, Benedict went to Rome to study. He was shocked by the corruption he found there and became a hermit. Others joined him and he eventually founded a monastery at Monte Cassino. Benedict's Rule, characterized by moderation and obedience, formed the basis of this order, and he became known as the father of Western monasticism.

Let the abbot aim to be loved rather than feared. He must not be worried or anxious, nor too exacting and harsh, nor jealous, or over-suspicious, for then he will never be at rest. He must temper everything so that the strong may not be held back and the weak not frightened off.

Let everything be done in moderation.

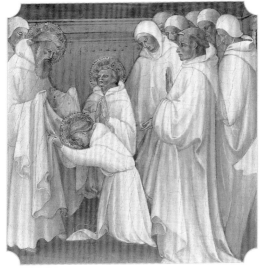

Lorenzo Monaco,
Saint Benedict admitting Saints Maurus
and Placidus into the Benedictine Order

Catherine

Feast day: November 25th

Catherine was a wealthy young woman from Alexandria, known for her beauty, learning and wit. The Roman emperor Maxentius asked her to marry him, but she refused, saying that she was already betrothed to Christ. In a rage he sentenced her to be broken on a spiked wheel. The wheel itself broke into pieces, injuring many bystanders, so Catherine was beheaded. The 'Catherine wheel' firework takes its name from this fourth-century event.

Now faith is the assurance of things hoped for; the conviction of things not seen... Let us hold fast to the confession of our hope without wavering, for he who has promised is faithful.

The New Testament letter to the Hebrews

Attributed to Garofalo,
Saint Catherine of Alexandria

Christopher

Feast day: July 25th

In the third century this man, known as Reprobus or Offero, reputedly offered to serve the devil, who appeared to him as a knight on a black horse. When the devil fled at the sight of a white cross, Reprobus decided to seek a more powerful master. A hermit set him the task of living near a river and carrying people across. One night, a child came to the river who was so heavy that Reprobus could hardly carry him. The child was Jesus Christ, weighed down with the sins of the world.

From that moment Reprobus took the name of Christopher, or Christ-bearer. He began to preach throughout Asia Minor, and was finally beheaded for refusing to sacrifice to Roman gods. There was a belief in medieval times that anyone who saw an image of Christopher would not die that day, and paintings of the saint with the Christ child on his back were hung beside church doors.

Style of the Master of the Female Half-Lengths,
Saint Christopher carrying the Infant Christ

Elizabeth

Feast day: November 5th

The cousin of Mary, Elizabeth was childless for many years until an angel appeared to her husband Zechariah and promised that a child would be born to them. This child was John the Baptist. When Mary came to visit, Elizabeth immediately recognized that God was at work in her life as well.

Blessed are you among women, and blessed is the fruit of your womb. And why has this happened to me, that the mother of my Lord comes to me? For as soon as I heard the sound of your greeting, the child in my womb leapt for joy. And blessed is she who believed that there would be a fulfilment of what was spoken to her by the Lord.

The Gospel of Luke

Workshop of the Master of 1518,
The Visitation of the Virgin to Saint Elizabeth

Francis

Feast day: October 4th

The son of a wealthy merchant, Francis became dissatisfied with worldly life and founded the Franciscan Order according to a simple rule based on sayings from the Gospels. Shortly before his death in 1226 he received the *stigmata* (marks of Christ's crucifixion) in his hands and side as a gift from God.

My God and my all.

Lord, make me an instrument of your peace. Where there is hatred, let me sow love.

Carlo Crivelli, Saint Franci.

Dominic

Feast day: August 8th

Contemporary with
Francis, Dominic was
the Spanish founder of
the Dominican Order.
Its members were also
known as the Friars
Preachers because of
their devotion to study
and preaching. Like
the Franciscans, they
practiced both individual
and corporate poverty
and lived by begging.

*A man who is ruler of
his passions is master of
the world.*

*I refuse to study dead skins
[books] while men are
dying of hunger.*

Carlo Crivelli, Saint Dominic

George

Little is known about this third-century soldier-saint who was beheaded for his faith. A famous legend tells how George saved Princess Cleolinda of Silene in Libya from a dragon. He tamed it and used her girdle to lead it back to the town, where he killed it. In Christian tradition the dragon can be a symbol of the devil; George is therefore seen as the champion of good over evil. At the time of the Crusades he was adopted as the patron saint of many countries, including Britain.

The great dragon was thrown down, that ancient serpent, who is called the Devil and Satan, the deceiver of the whole world. Then I heard a loud voice in heaven, proclaiming, 'Now have come the salvation and the power and the kingdom of our God and the authority of his Messiah.'

The Book of Revelation

Paolo Uccello,
Saint George and the Dragon

James

Feast day: July 25th

Sometimes known as Saint James the Great, James left the family fishing business together with his brother John to follow Jesus. In AD 44 he was executed by King Herod Agrippa, becoming one of the first disciples to die for his faith. A seventh-century legend tells how he preached the gospel in Spain, and his shrine at Santiago di Compostela has since become one of the great centers of pilgrimage in the West.

Jesus saw two brothers, James son of Zebedee and his brother John, in the boat with their father Zebedee, mending their nets, and he called them. Immediately they left the boat and their father, and followed him.

The Gospel of Matthew

*Workshop of the Master of the Saint Bartholomew Altarpiece,
Saint James the Great*

Jerome

Feast day: September 30th

Jerome was a great fourth-century scholar who wrote many biblical commentaries, and whose Latin revision and retranslation of the Bible was later collected into what became known as the Vulgate. He spent four or five years as a hermit in the Syrian desert, becoming an inspiration for Christian penitents and hermits. According to legend, Jerome removed a thorn from a lion's paw, and the lion became his friend from that time onwards.

Lord, thou hast given us thy word for a light to shine upon our path; grant us so to meditate on that word, and to follow its teaching, that we may find in it the light that shines more and more until the perfect day; through Jesus Christ our Lord.

Plato located the soul of man in the head, Christ located it in the heart.

Vincenzo Catena,
Saint Jerome in his Study

John the Baptist
Feast days: June 24th, August 29th

Prophet, preacher and baptizer, John was the first to recognize his cousin Jesus as 'the Lamb of God'. Imprisoned for his preaching by King Herod, he was beheaded in around AD 30 as the result of a plot by Queen Herodias and her daughter Salome.

This is the one of whom the prophet Isaiah spoke when he said, 'The voice of one crying out in the wilderness: "Prepare the way of the Lord, make his paths straight." '

I baptize you with water for repentance, but one who is more powerful than I is coming after me. He will baptize you with the Holy Spirit and fire.

The Gospel of Matthew

Pierre-Cécile Puvis de Chavannes,
The Beheading of Saint John the Baptist

John

Feast day: December 27th

Possibly the youngest of Jesus' disciples, John is
traditionally believed to be the author of the Gospel
of John, the three Epistles of John and possibly
the Book of Revelation, and is variously known
as Saint John the Evangelist, Saint John of Patmos
or Saint John the Divine. He described himself
as 'the disciple whom Jesus loved'.

*I looked, and there was a great multitude that no one
could count, from every nation, from all tribes and
peoples and languages, standing before the throne and
before the Lamb, robed in white, with palm branches
in their hands. They cried out in a loud voice, saying,
'Salvation belongs to our God who is seated on the
throne, and to the Lamb!'*

The Book of Revelation

South German,
Saint John on Patmos

Joseph

Feast days: March 19th, May 1st

Husband of Mary and foster-father of Jesus, Joseph was a builder and a carpenter. It is probable that he died before Jesus began his traveling ministry.

Joseph, son of David, do not be afraid to take Mary as your wife, for the child conceived in her is from the Holy Spirit. She will bear a son, and you are to name him Jesus, for he will save his people from their sins.

The Gospel of Matthew

Philippe de Champaigne,
The Vision of Saint Joseph

Lawrence

Feast day: August 10th

In the third century the Prefect of the city of Rome demanded that the church hand over all its wealth. Lawrence, deacon to Pope Sixtus II, gathered together thousands of the poor, sick and old people in his care and delivered them to the Prefect, saying, 'The church is truly rich, far richer than your Emperor.' He was burned to death on a gridiron.

Do not store up for yourselves treasures on earth, where moth and rust consume and where thieves break in and steal; but store up for yourselves treasures in heaven. For where your treasure is, there your heart will be also.

The Gospel of Matthew

Circle of the Master of the Legend of Saint Ursula,
Saint Lawrence showing the Prefect the Treasures of the Church

Luke

Feast day: October 18th

Luke was a doctor from Antioch in Syria. He traveled with Paul, recording their journeys in the book known as the Acts of the Apostles. This was a continuation of his Gospel account in which he focused on the story of Jesus' life. According to legend, Luke painted the Virgin and Child and thus is known as the patron saint of painters.

Since many have undertaken to set down an orderly account of the events that have been fulfilled among us, just as they were handed on to us by those who from the beginning were eyewitnesses and servants of the word, I too decided to write an orderly account for you, most excellent Theophilus, so that you may know the truth concerning the things about which you have been instructed.

The Gospel of Luke

Follower of Massys,
Saint Luke painting the Virgin and Child

Mary

Feast day: January 1st

Mary lived in Nazareth in northern Israel, and legend names her parents as Anne and Joachim. She was engaged to Joseph, a local builder and carpenter, when the Angel Gabriel appeared to her to announce that she would become the mother of Christ by the Holy Spirit.

My soul magnifies the Lord, and my spirit rejoices in God my Savior; for he has looked with favor on the lowliness of his servant. Surely, from now on all generations will call me blessed; for the Mighty One has done great things for me, and holy is his name.

The Gospel of Luke

Raphael,
The Madonna and Child with the Infant Baptist

Mary Magdalene
Feast day: July 22nd

Jesus healed Mary of demon possession, and she became one of his closest friends. She stood with the other women at the cross when Jesus died, and was one of the first to see him after his resurrection.

Mary stood weeping outside the tomb. She turned round and saw Jesus standing there, but she did not know that it was Jesus. Jesus said to her, 'Woman, why are you weeping? For whom are you looking?' Supposing him to be the gardener, she said to him, 'Sir, if you have carried him away, tell me where you have laid him, and I will take him away.' Jesus said to her, 'Mary!'

The Gospel of John

Gian Girolamo Savoldo,
Saint Mary Magdalene approaching the Sepulchre

Matthew

Feast day: September 21st

A swindling and hated tax collector, Matthew, originally called Levi, became one of the first apostles and a gospel writer.

As Jesus was walking along, he saw a man called Matthew sitting at the tax booth; and he said to him, 'Follow me.' And he got up and followed him.

The Gospel of Matthew

Stephan Lochner,
Saint Matthew

Mark

Feast day: April 25th

A young man at the time of Jesus, Mark may well have been the person who fled naked from Gethsemane when Christ was arrested. He later traveled with Paul and Barnabas.

Only Luke is with me. Get Mark and bring him with you, for he is useful in my ministry.

Paul's second letter to Timothy

Cima da Conegliano, Saint Mark (?)

Paul

Feast days: January 25th, June 29th

Paul, originally Saul, became a Christian after seeing a vision of Jesus on the road to Damascus. Known as the Apostle to the Gentiles, he was the church's greatest missionary and most influential theologian, and many of his pastoral letters are included in the New Testament. He is believed to have died in Rome around AD 65.

Love is patient; love is kind; love is not envious or boastful or arrogant or rude. It does not insist on its own way; it is not irritable or resentful; it does not rejoice in wrongdoing, but rejoices in the truth. It bears all things, believes all things, hopes all things, endures all things. Love never ends.

Paul's first letter to the Corinthians

Pier Francesco Sacchi,
Saint Paul Writing

Simon Peter

Feast day: June 29th

A leader among the twelve apostles, Simon was renamed Peter (or 'rock') by Jesus. According to tradition, he and his wife traveled throughout Asia Minor preaching the gospel. Finally he went to Rome, where he was crucified upside-down and buried on the spot where the high altar of Saint Peter's Basilica now stands in the Vatican.

'I tell you, when you were younger, you used to fasten your own belt and to go wherever you wished. But when you grow old, you will stretch out your hands, and someone else will fasten a belt around you and take you where you do not wish to go.' (Jesus said this to indicate the kind of death by which Peter would glorify God.)

The Gospel of John

Master of the Palazzo Venezia Madonna,
Saint Peter

Thomas

Feast day: July 3rd

One of the twelve apostles, Thomas is believed to have traveled to India, where he founded a church. An ancient cross marks his burial place near Madras. Thomas is sometimes known as Doubting Thomas because he asked to see Jesus' wounds before he would believe in the resurrection.

Although the doors were shut, Jesus came and stood among them and said, 'Peace be with you.' Then he said to Thomas, 'Put your finger here and see my hands. Reach out your hand and put it in my side. Do not doubt but believe.' Thomas answered him, 'My Lord and my God!'

The Gospel of John

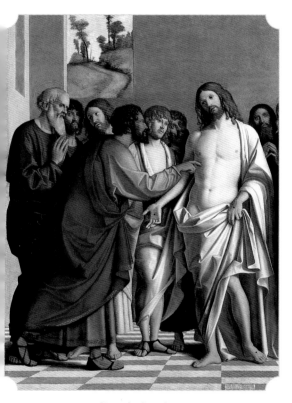

Cima da Conegliano,
The Incredulity of Saint Thomas

Text acknowledgments

5: 1 Corinthians 13:3. 8: John 1:41–42. 12: Hebrews 11:1, 10:23. 16: Luke
1:42–45. 20: Revelation 12:9–10. 22: Matthew 4:21–22. 26: Matthew 3:3, 11.
28: Revelation 7:9–10. 30: Matthew 1:20–21. 32: Matthew 6:19–21. 34: Luke
1:1–4. 36: Luke 1:46–49. 38: John 20:11, 14–16. 40: Matthew 9:9. 41: 2 Timothy
4:11. 42: 1 Corinthians 13:4–8. 44: John 21:18–19. 46: John 20:26–28.

Scripture quotations are taken from The New Revised Standard Version of the Bible,
Anglicized Edition, copyright © 1989, 1995 by the Division of Christian Education
of the National Council of the Churches of Christ in the United States of America,
and are used by permission. All rights reserved. Spelling and punctuation of quotations
may have been modernized.

Picture acknowledgments

All pictures in this book are details. Copyright © The National Gallery, London.

Cover, 12–13: NG 3118 Saint Catherine of Alexandria, attributed to Garofalo.
8–9: NG 3925 Saint Andrew (?), Gaudenzio Ferrari. 10–11: NG 2862 Saint
Benedict admitting Saints Maurus and Placidus into the Benedictine Order,
Lorenzo Monaco. 14–15: NG 716 Saint Christopher carrying the Infant Christ,
style of the Master of the Female Half-Lengths. 16–17: NG 1082 The Visitation
of the Virgin to Saint Elizabeth, Workshop of the Master of 1518. 18: NG 788.6
Saint Francis, Carlo Crivelli. 19: NG 788.5 Saint Dominic, Carlo Crivelli. 20–21:
NG 6294 Saint George and the Dragon, Paolo Uccello. 22–23: NG 6497 The
Virgin and Child in Glory with Saint James the Great and Saint Cecilia, Workshop
of the Master of the Saint Bartholomew Altarpiece. 24–25: NG 694 Saint Jerome
in his Study, Vincenzo Catena. 26–27: NG 3266 The Beheading of Saint John the
Baptist, Pierre-Cécile Puvis de Chavannes. 28–29: NG 4901 Saint John on Patmos,
South German. 30–31: NG 6276 The Vision of Saint Joseph, Philippe de Champaigne.
32–33: NG 3665 Saint Lawrence showing the Prefect the Treasures of the Church,
Circle of the Master of the Legend of Saint Ursula. 34–35: NG 3902 Saint Luke
painting the Virgin and Child, follower of Massys. 36–37: NG 744 The Madonna
and Child with the Infant Baptist (The Garvagh Madonna), Raphael. 38–39: NG
1031 Saint Mary Magdalene approaching the Sepulchre, Gian Girolamo Savoldo.
40: NG 705 Saints Matthew, Catherine of Alexandria and John the Evangelist,
Stephan Lochner. 41: NG 4945 Saint Mark (?), Giovanni Battista Cima da
Conegliano. 42–43: NG 3944 Saint Paul Writing, Pier Francesco Sacchi. 44–45:
NG 4492 Saint Peter, Master of the Palazzo Venezia Madonna. 46–47: NG 816
The Incredulity of Saint Thomas, Giovanni Battista Cima da Conegliano.